PIANO

Listen & Learn
HOMESPUN MUSIC INSTRUCTION

AUDIO ACCESS INCLUDED

DR. JOHN
TEACHES
New Orleans Piano
—— VOLUME 1 ——
In-Depth Sessions with a Master Musician

T0053159

PLAYBACK+
Speed • Pitch • Balance • Loop

To access audio online, visit:
www.halleonard.com/mylibrary

Enter Code
7905-9377-0980-8534

Cover Photo by Chris Rials-Seitz

Audio Editors: George James and Ted Orr

Mastered by: Ted Orr at
Nevessa Productions, Woodstock, NY

Produced by Happy Traum for Homespun Tapes

ISBN 978-0-7935-8170-2

HOMESPUN®

EXCLUSIVELY DISTRIBUTED BY

HAL•LEONARD®
7777 W. BLUEMOUND RD. P.O. BOX 13819 MILWAUKEE, WI 53213

© 1997 HOMESPUN TAPES LTD.
BOX 340
WOODSTOCK, NY 12498-0694
All Rights Reserved

Visit Hal Leonard Online at **www.halleonard.com**

Visit Homespun Tapes at **www.homespun.com**

Audio instruction makes it easy! Find the section of the lesson you want with the press of a finger; play that segment over and over until you've mastered it; easily skip over parts you've already mastered; listen with the best possible audio fidelity; follow along track-by-track with the book.

Table of Contents

PAGE	AUDIO TRACK	
4	1	Opening Music
4	1	"Texas Boogie" and Introduction

Boogie Styles

PAGE	AUDIO TRACK	
7	2	"Texas Boogie"– Broken Down
8	3	Albert Ammons Boogie
8	4	Boogie Bass Lines
12	5	"Cow Cow Boogie"
14	6	Professor Longhair
16	7	"Frankie and Johnny"
19	8	Boogie Turnarounds and Rhythms

12-Bar Blues

PAGE	AUDIO TRACK	
21	9	12-Bar Blues – "C.C. Rider"
23	10	Turnarounds

8-Bar Blues

PAGE	AUDIO TRACK	
26	11	"How Long"
26	12	New Orleans 8-Bar – "Blues"
28	13	Basic 8-Bar Blues

Professor Longhair

PAGE	AUDIO TRACK	
31	14	Professor Longhair Style
32	15	"Big Chief"
36	16	"Down by the Riverside" (Mardi Gras Indian Influence)

Set-Ups and Turnarounds

PAGE	AUDIO TRACK	
38	17	"Whirlaway" (Alan Toussaint)
38	18	Set-Ups and Turnarounds
39	19	"Dr. John's Turnaround Tune"

◆1 "Texas Boogie" and Introduction

Texas Boogie

That's a little bit of the "Texas Boogie." That's me, Dr. John, The Night Tripper playing it for you. That's the first boogie-woogie I learned back in the '40s from various people in my family.

It's a very simple boogie due to the fact that both hands play in unison rhythms. I learned it in New Orleans when I was a young child, maybe six or seven years old.

I took lessons when I was a teenager, but I already knew basically how to play before I took lessons. I took guitar lessons when I was 12 or 13. I already knew a little about the guitar and I would sit at home and practice guitar with Lightnin' Hopkins records. But I didn't know anything about structured guitar music, so I took lessons at Werlein's music store in New Orleans from a guy named Al Guma, who had studied with Walter "Papoose" Nelson, who was Fats Domino's guitar player, and Roy Montrell, who later became Fats Domino's guitar player. All three of them, Guma, Montrell and Papoose, taught me totally different styles and thoughts about the instrument.

Papoose mostly taught me how to comp for people so that it would drive the band.

Roy Montrell taught me that it was important to know various voicings of chords.

I was able to apply the guitar knowledge I had to the piano. A lot of the music I learned criss-crosses back and forth.

Boogie Styles

"Texas Boogie"–Breakdown

The "Texas Boogie" starts out with both hands playing rhythmically together. You keep playing the same patterns as you switch from the C chord to the F7 chord.

❷ Texas Boogie – Broken Down

As you go along you just add a little to it.

It all comes out of the simple little idea you started with.

The left hand stays in the same basic rhythm throughout:

❸ Albert Ammons Boogie

The "Texas Boogie" is more of a blues boogie than, say, Albert Ammons' stuff, which is real boogie-woogie.

The difference is mostly in the left hand, which, in the Albert Ammons boogie-woogie style, plays a more complex line.

❹ Boogie Bass Lines

Here are each of the left-hand examples on the recording written out.

The first boogie woogie left-hand example is:

Boogie Example – left hand only

The second boogie left-hand pattern is like a walking bass, with the notes walking in moving octaves:

Walking Bass – played one octave lower

With the walking bass, you can walk any pattern or sequence of notes that is within a chord structure and it will work. It gives you a lot more freedom. A lot of guys I've heard over the years have said that when they're doing something very difficult with their right hand, they might just play repeating octaves in the left hand, and not even move it, like the following example:

(Play one octave lower than written)

You can move it very simply to the next chord:

(Play one octave lower than written)

The walking bass is a very useful type of left-hand pattern.

The walking bass is also the basis for such tunes as the "Mess Around" and the "Cow Cow Boogie," 2/4 boogies that go in this kind of sequence.

$\frac{2}{4}$ Boogie with Walking Bass

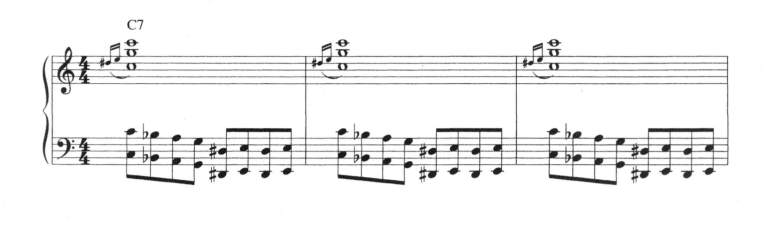

One of the values of the walking bass line is that, with a subtle rhythmic change,
it feels more like a 2/4 rhythm rather than a straight 4/4 boogie rhythm.

You know I've played this kind of thing for many years:

"Cow Cow Boogie"
Mess Around

What you have there is the basic 2/4 boogie, the "Cow Cow Boogie," or "Mess Around." A lot of people, Cow Cow Davenport, Paul Gaylen and Ray Charles have played that. It's near and dear to my heart because of the 2/4 rhythm being such a New Orleans feeling rhythm.

What you have there is a 2/4 against a 4/4 feeling. A drummer could play that both ways. One of the basic elements of the New Orleans piano style is that two rhythms can go on simultaneously, one inside the other.

◆ **6 Professor Longhair**

One of the natural elements of this style is to try to set-up each chord change with a pattern that lets the listeners know a change is coming up.

Here's a Professor Longhair-type set-up:

Professor Longhair Setup

Here's a Huey "Piano" Smith-type set-up:

Hughie "Piano" Smith Setup

Here's a standard New Orleans-style set-up:

Standard New Orleans Setup

I do more of Professor Longhair's stuff than anyone else because I feel that he was, as Alan Toussaint so eloquently put it, "The Bach of Rock," and the godfather of funk rhythms as well as the traditional New Orleans rhythms. Professor Longhair took the old shuffling rhythm style that Fats Domino put on so many records,

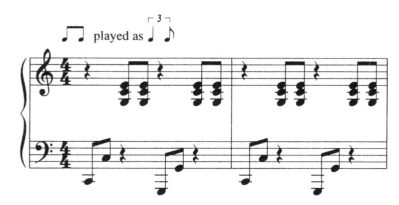

and it became something more like the following example:

Professor Longhair was able to use the piano as several rhythm instruments rather than just one rhythm instrument, like he also has a guitar part and a drum part in the piano part.

A very important part of the concept of New Orleans-style piano is that the piano is a rhythm instrument and a melodic instrument, but also an instrument to tie up the band and lead the band, as well as an instrument that keeps the band sounding full.

⑦ "Frankie and Johnny"

A song like "Frankie and Johnny" is a good song to demonstrate turnarounds to go from one chord to another. This also happens at the end of one chorus to go to the top of another chorus.

"Frankie and Johnny"

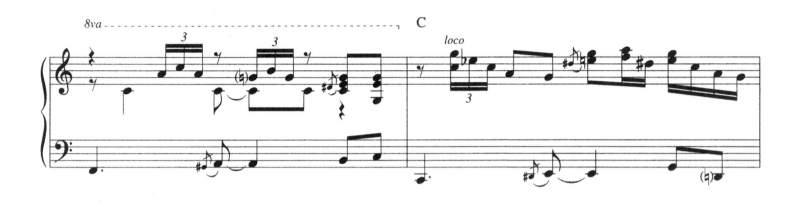

Three Set-ups–I to IV chord:

A.

B. Contrary Motion

etc.

C.

❽ Boogie Turnarounds and Rhythms

The use of turnarounds is always to set up the next chord or the top of a new chorus.

End of Chorus Setup

Walk Up – I to IV Chord

That pattern sets up the drum rhythm to play the "second line" rhythm in New Orleans style music.

The basic difference I've heard between Chicago pianists and Texas pianists and New Orleans pianists is that the New Orleans piano player's hand leans with the snare drum a lot. A lot of times you'll hear Professor Longhair or Eurreal "Little Brother" Montgomery playing things like:

This is like the drums playing ruffs. The piano player helps set up a natural drum rhythm and cushions the drummer as he plays his ruffs.

I think it has a lot to do with drummers back in the days when upright bass players weren't heard as well on gigs. It's a natural rhythm that helps the group lock in on something. It's a natural rhythm. It cushions the guys playing. The bass and drums have an easy time playing with rhythms like that. The rhythms of the bass, drums and guitar can all be established by the piano.

◆⑨ 12-Bar Blues – "C.C. Rider"

This is an example of the "C.C. Rider"-type of 12-bar blues.

12-Bar Blues
C.C. Rider Type

That's your very basic 12-bar blues. I tried to play it without any frills, in order to demonstrate some very simple turnarounds we consistently use.

⑩ Turnarounds

Here's a basic turnaround:

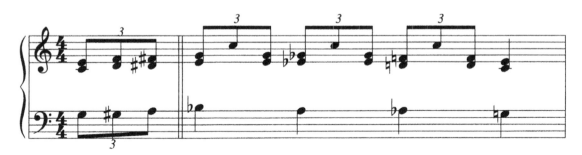

The basic turnaround can be embellished on:

Embellished

Or embellished further with tenths in the left hand:

Tenths in bass

Each way you play it would be appropriate in a certain type of setting. If you're playing with a band and you're trying to keep the piano within a certain register, the first way might be most appropriate.

If it's a smaller group and you want to spread the voicing, play the embellished turnaround.

If you're playing solo piano, you might want to play the tenths in the left hand to fill it out.

The tenths imply the whole harmony. An important part of playing solo piano is, not necessarily to do everything and to get overly busy, but to make the harmony sound full. Tenths work well for that.

If you're going to play the blues, you should learn as many turnaround as possible. A great percentage of blues music is based on the turnaround.

Progressive Style

It's still a basic 12-bar blues turnaround. The progressive turnaround merely uses more substitute chords. Within a blues, you can play as many substitute chords as you like, as long as it relates to the song you're playing. For instance, within the blues, you don't want to hear major seventh and major ninth chords, like you would hear in a more pop ballad style. In the blues, you want to hear dominant sevenths and minor sevenths. That makes it more bluesy. I've never really approved of the guys who play the chords to "Bluesette" within a blues structure. "Bluesette" is a nice piece unto itself, but it's not really appropriate in a true blues structure.

⓫ "How Long"

Let's put down an 8-bar blues form, "How Long."

That's a very traditional blues pattern. You can play any of the 8-bar blues patterns in various ways. For example, you could even vary the first three chords. One of the beautiful things about playing these songs is that there's almost no limit as to the actual chords you can use within the structure as long as the chords work with the melody.

⓬ New Orleans 8-Bar – "Blues"

The New Orleans 8-bar blues style is like Professor Longhair's "Tipitina," which is the kind of blues I'm more familiar with playing.

New Orleans 8-Bar Blues

It starts out with a series of ruffs.

That's a very traditional New Orleans style 8-bar blues. As you can hear, the basic difference is that it's not straight rhythmically. It's a combination of calypso, Latin rhythms and Afro-Caribbean rhythms mixed with a straight-ahead blues rhythm. The 8-bar blues is much more akin to a lot of the New Orleans music.

◆13 Basic 8-Bar Blues

This is your basic 8-bar blues style in its most basic form, with the basic trills in the right hand between the third and the fifth.

8-Bar Blues

The left-hand pattern is very basic.

The left hand and the trills in the right hand, those are your trademarks of a
certain style of 8-bar blues.

◆14 Professor Longhair Style

One of the characteristics of Professor Longhair's style is using ruffs, with the drummer:

The left hand could be played very straight, for instance:

However, the left hand doesn't necessarily have to be played that straight. It could be played:

You can use the left hand to accent some of the right-hand parts.

I worked as Professor Longhair's guitarist both on sessions and on gigs, also as his bass player at times, but mostly as his guitarist. We had the good fortune in the 50s and 60s to hear him sit down on the drums and play for the drummer what he wanted the drummer to play, or to show me on the guitar what he wanted me to play. This was a great advantage over the guys who worked with him later.

He had a unique way of expressing himself verbally. For instance, when the horns play what we call a "fall off," he called that a "spew." And he called the foot pedals on the drums "foot propedellers." He used real descriptive words. Like when I got too much distortion on the guitar, he called it "extortion." He said one time, that someone had composed a song, but that he had "decomposed" it. He gave all the guys that worked with him a double interest in the music, both by his picturesque way of describing the music and by his dynamic way of playing things.

◆15 "Big Chief"

Professor Longhair recorded "Big Chief" around 1963 or '64. "Big Chief" was a song Earl King wrote for him, but Professor Longhair created a completely new rhythm and melody for the song. He had already created "Tipitina," which established the way the New Orleans 8-bar blues went. And he had created 16-bar blues like "Mardi Gras In New Orleans," which became the Mardi Gras anthem every year. "Tipitina" was kind of an Afro-Caribbean rhythm and "Mardi Gras In New Orleans" was a very specific mambo rhythm.

"Big Chief" was the anthem of the Mardi Gras Indians in New Orleans. The song changed the rhythmic structure of music to what we have today, what we call the funk rhythm.

Big Chief

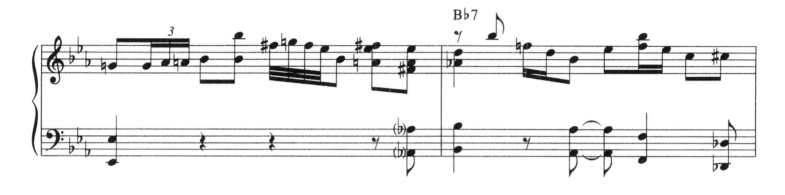

This piece changed the pattern of bass lines to a more syncopated rhythm, like the kind you hear in records today.

Professor Longhair changed the shuffle rhythm to an eighth note rhythm. And in this piece he changed the eighth note rhythm to syncopated sixteenth notes, which became the emblem of all disco music and the funk style.

When you hear Professor Longhair play this right hand part,

Big Chief R.H.

note the use of fourths and also the major and minor thirds implied into it.

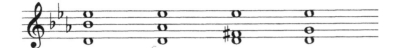

This was a rhythm that hadn't been used in blues, or rhythm and blues or rock and roll up to that time. When you put the parts together, it becomes something unique. Professor Longhair also captured the Mardi Gras Indians' rhythmic concept, like in the song "Iko Iko," recorded by the Neville Brothers, the Grateful Dead, myself, the Dixie Cups and others. That song has been in the charts four or five times throughout the years. It's a song that typifies the carnival spirit of the Mardi Gras Indians of New Orleans.

◆16 "Down by The Riverside" (Mardi Gras Indian Influence)

Take a great old gospel tune like "Down By The Riverside." Songs like this fit in the Mardi Gras Indians tradition, but they have this particular rhythm:

Some people know it as the "Bo Diddley" rhythm or the "shave and a haircut, two bits" rhythm. This is a very essential part of what the Mardi Gras Indians use as a basic rhythm which goes along with what we call the "second line" rhythm of New Orleans, which in "Down By The Riverside" is:

"Down By The Riverside" Second Line Rhythm

8ba throughout

The Indians combine the two rhythms together, so you get something like the following:

8ba throughout

36

That's what we call a *gumbo* in New Orleans, putting a little bit of this and a little bit of that and, if it's something to eat, it tastes good, and if it's something to dance to, it feels good to dance to. It's such a great rhythm that you can't help but get out of your chair and do whatever makes you feel good.

Gumbo

8va throughout

etc.

Songs like "Big Chief" became anthems for whole segments of the community of New Orleans and helped pull the city together through a time of race troubles and things. This type of music serves a higher purpose by helping pull the community together in spirit.

Set-Ups And Turnarounds

⑰ "Whirlaway" (Allen Toussaint)

I'll give you an example of how you can use a rhythmic thing to set up the chord change. This is a little Allen Toussaint song called "Whirlaway."

⑱ Set-ups and Turnarounds

What I was doing there was setting up each chord change *á la* Professor Longhair (even though this is an Allen Toussaint song) with this kind of set-up.

A: "Walk up" to IV Chord   **B: Contrary Motion**

When you hear that, it's very, very obvious that a chord change is coming.

Here's another set-up:

All these set-ups are used typically in New Orleans music to indicate chord changes. They are also used at the ends of choruses to set up the next chorus, like the following:

Note: Play entire example one octave lower than written.

You can't miss that something else is going to happen after that.

It's very important in that it lets the drummer and the bass and the people that are dancing know that something's coming. It helps the people on the dance floor lock in community-style. It gives them time to adjust. It helps the drummer relax.

One of the misconceptions I've always heard drummers say about New Orleans music is that it's played late or that it's played back in the time. But actually, how it's played is that it's *relaxed*. That's the key to being rhythmically laid back, not to play late, but to play *relaxed*, no matter how driving or exciting the rhythm is.

⟨19⟩ "Dr. John's Turnaround Tune"

To give a solid example of how important these turnarounds and set-ups are to music as a whole, I'll show how a whole song can be constructed from a single turnaround. This is a song I wrote, which is based on a Huey Smith turnaround:

Turnaround Tune

That whole song is based on this single turnaround:

Whatever way these turnarounds and set-ups are used, they have the purpose of setting up what's to come.

That's about it for this volume. This is Dr. John, the Night Tripper. See you in Volume 2.

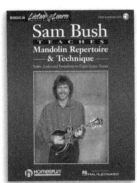

SAM BUSH TEACHES MANDOLIN REPERTOIRE & TECHNIQUE

One of the most versatile and powerful musicians playing today teaches 8 great repertoire tunes that will help mandolin players develop their style and technique. This lesson covers traditional bluegrass tunes as well as jazz-flavored "new-grass" originals: Cotton Patch Rag • Tom & Jerry • Leather Britches • Lime Rock • Banjalin • Diadem • Norman and Nancy • and Russian Rag.

00695339 Book/Online Audio.....................$19.99

RUSS BARENBERG TEACHES 20 BLUEGRASS GUITAR SOLOS

REPERTOIRE TUNES FOR INTERMEDIATE PLAYERS
One of America's top bluegrass guitarists teaches a variety of flatpicking solos for twenty favorite songs and instrumentals. Played slowed-down and up-to-speed for learning players, with rhythm tracks availble for download or streaming online for great practice sessions. Songs: Liberty • Soldier's Joy • Forked Deer • Eighth of January • Hot Corn, Cold Corn • Down Yonder • John Henry • Blackberry Blossom • Leather Britches • and more. Level 3

00695220 Book/Online Audio................................$19.99

PAUL BUTTERFIELD – BLUES HARMONICA MASTER CLASS

Paul Butterfield was an original and groundbreaking blues harmonica player who brought acoustic Delta blues playing into the electrified blues/rock scene pioneered by Muddy Waters, Little Walter and others. In this rare instructional book with online audio instruction, he teaches many of the techniques that made him famous: note- bending, tongue-blocking and tremolo, as well as many great blues licks and tricks.

00699089 Book/Online Audio.....................$19.99

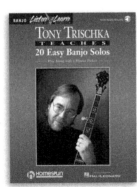

TONY TRISCHKA EASY BANJO SOLOS

Strengthen your skills while building a repertoire of great bluegrass banjo pieces! Tony Trischka has personally chosen twenty traditional banjo solos that will teach you new ideas and add to your arsenal of licks and techniques. On the online audio, Tony performs each tune slowly, then up to speed, providing invaluable tips and explanations as he goes. By the time you have mastered all of these solos, you'll have acquired the basic skills necessary to play in the styles of Earl Scruggs, Don Reno, Sonny Osborne, and other bluegrass greats.

00699056 Book/Online Audio................................$19.99

STEVE KAUFMAN'S FOUR-HOUR BLUEGRASS WORKOUT

with Bennie Boling (banjo)
Here's a great way to improve your picking, build up speed and stamina, and get those licks and solos working – no matter what instrument you play! Whether you are a professional or a "parking lot" player, these fabulous sessions will get your fingers in shape – fast! On the four CDs, you have a dedicated bluegrass band playing rhythm to give you solid back-up to 49 great tunes, both slowed-down and up-to-speed. Steve plays the lead parts so you can learn to solo with a band.

00641379 Book/CD Pack...$44.95

TONY TRISCHKA – BANJO BUNDLE PACK

Tony Trischka Teaches 20 Easy Banjo Solos (00699056) and the DVD *Classic Bluegrass Banjo Solos* (00641567) in one money-saving pack. You'll get hours of in-depth banjo instruction from one of the world's best players and teachers, and will learn the licks, solos and techniques of the great historical pickers: Scruggs, Stanley, Reno, et al.

00642060 Book/CD/DVD Pack....................$44.95

ALL STAR BLUEGRASS JAM ALONG

BACKUPS, LEAD PARTS AND NOTE-FOR-NOTE TRANSCRIPTIONS FOR 21 ESSENTIAL TUNES
featuring Todd Phillips
Book/CD Packs

These fabulous collections for players of all levels feature 21 must-know bluegrss songs & instrumentals, created especially for learning players by the genre's leading artists. The artist plays a basic solo that states the melody of the tune, then a more adventurous improvisation, and each solo is transcribed in detail. The CD provides the audio versions of the solos, plus multiple rhythm tracks performed at moderate tempo for easy play-along. This great series will help you build your repertoire & get your licks in shape, so you can shine in your next performance or jam session! Songs include: Bill Cheatham • Blackberry Blossom • Down in the Willow Garden • I Am a Pilgrim • I'll Fly Away • In the Pines • John Hardy • Old Joe Clark • Soldier's Joy • more!

00641947 Bass	....	$19.95
00641943 Guitar	....	$19.95
00641946 Fiddle	....	$19.95
00641945 Mandolin	....	$19.95
00641944 Banjo	....	$19.95

Prices, contents and availability subject to change without notice.